THE WAY WE WERE

CALIFORNIA

Nostalgic Images of the Golden State

THE WAY WE WERE

CALIFORNIA

Nostalgic Images of the Golden State

M. J. Howard & Laurie Mayer

gpp

Guilford, Connecticut

To buy books in quantity for corporate use or incentives, call (800) 962-0973 or e-mail premiums@GlobePequot.com.

Design: Compendium design/Angela and Dave Ball
Editor: Joshua Rosenberg
Photo credits: All photographs, unless specified below, are from the Library of Congress Prints & Photographs Division. Corbis: 1 (Henry G. Peabody), 4 (Michael Ochs Archives), 9 (Arnold Genthe), 11B (Robert L. Bracklow), 13BR (Philip Gendreau), 14 (Michael Ochs Archives), 15T (Michael Ochs Archives), 16 (Aladdin Color, Inc.), 24 (Lake County Museum), 29B (Historical Collection), 31 (William Carroll), 34 (Allen Ginsberg), 36T (Lake County Museum), 36B (Horace Bristol), 38L (Galen Rowell), 38R (Spirit), 39 (John Springer Collection), 42 (Michael Ochs Archives), 43 (Michael Childers/Sygma), 48 (C. Moore), 49 (Philip James Corwin), 54 (Historical Collection), 55B (Hulton-Deutsch Collection), 56BR (Roger Ressmeyer), 59B (Historical Collection), 61 (Kurt Hutton), 62–63 (Arthur Rothstein), 64 (Hulton-Deutsch Collection), 66 (Lake County Museum), 67 (Carleton E. Watkins), 68–69 (MedioImages), 71 (Arthur Rothstein), 72 (Thomas A. Heinz), 73 (Richard Bryant/Arcaid), 76 (E.O. Hoppé), 78 (Phil Schermeister), 80 (Underwood & Underwood), 81 (G.E. Kidder Smith/Hearst Castle/CA Park Service), 85 (Michael Ochs Archives), 87 (Alan Weintraub/Arcaid), 91 (Michael Ochs Archives), 95 (Horace Bristol), 96 (Leland J. Prater), 97T (Underwood & Underwood), 99 (Robert Landau), 100L (Underwood & Underwood), 101R (Photo Media/ClassicStock), 117 (Henry G. Peabody), 122 (Michael Ochs Archives), 125T (Henry Diltz), 125B (Henry Diltz), 127T (Richard Cummins), 127B (Nik Wheeler). Bettmann/Corbis: 8L, 13BL, 15B, 30, 32, 33T, 33B, 35, 37, 40, 41, 44, 45, 50T, 50B, 56T, 56BL, 57, 58, 59T, 60T, 60B, 65T, 74T, 74B, 75, 80–81, 82, 83L, 83R (Bob Flora/UPI), 84, 86, 88 , 89T, 89B, 77, 90 (Dave Cicero), 92, 93, 94, 97B, 98, 100R, 101TL, 101BL, 104, 105B, 107, 110, 112L, 112TR, 112BR, 113T, 113B, 114TR, 115T, 115B, 118, 119T, 119B, 120, 121L, 121R, 111 (Bill Hormell), 123, 124L (Philip Gendreau), 124R (Philip Gendreau), 126

Library of Congress Cataloging-in-Publication Data

Howard, M. J. (Martin J.)
The way we were California : nostalgic images of the Golden State / M.J. Howard & Laurie Mayer.
p. cm.
Includes index.
ISBN 978-0-7627-5452-6
1. California--History--Pictorial works. 2. California--Social life and customs--Pictorial works. I. Mayer, Laurie (Laurie Suzanne) II. Title.
F862.H69 2009
979.4'053--dc22

2009026060

Printed in China

10 9 8 7 6 5 4 3 2 1

CONTENTS

INTRODUCTION

The state of California is a place like no other, a place of bewildering contrasts in scenery, culture, and even climate. Its cities are as distinct from one another as the people who live in them, its natural splendors virtually a world in microcosm. Here you will find the Alpine peaks of the Sierra Nevada and—in the Mojave and Colorado—two distinct types of desert. California also has luxuriant forests, beaches and rugged coastline, sweeping vineyards and orchards, hissing volcanic fumaroles and belching mud pots, along with plant and animal species not found anywhere else on the planet. It is a place drenched in sunshine with a liberal sprinkling of razzle-dazzle, where dreams come true and legends are born, and where a fascinating assortment of folks live side by side. Over the years it has attracted people of every stripe, from starry-eyed fortune seekers to Nobel Prize winners and technological wizards, from pioneer farmers to industrial magnates. And while many non-

"California has become the first American state where there is no majority race, and we're doing just fine. If you look around the room, you can see a microcosm of what we can do in the world. . . . You should be hopeful on balance about the future. But it's like any future since the beginning of time—you're going to have to make it."

Bill Clinton

OPPOSITE AND ABOVE: North of San Diego is the "Jewel of the California Missions," San Juan Capistrano. It was founded on All Saints Day, November 1, 1776. A chapel here is the oldest building in California still in regular use. San Juan Capistrano also holds the distinction of having introduced viniculture to California. But what it is truly loved for is "The Miracle of the Swallows." Every year on St. Joseph's Day, March 19, the flock of migrating swallows make their way back to the mission to begin rebuilding their mud nests on the old stone church. Visitors from all over the world gather each year to witness the miracle of the swallows' return, and celebrate the *Festival de las Golondrinas*.

ABOVE: California's first church and first of the twenty-one Spanish missions built along the coast was the Mission San Diego de Alcala, which dates to 1769. The original building was burned to the ground by rioting Natives in 1775, but by the end of the eighteenth century, the mission was firmly established with thousands of Native American converts farming 50,000 acres.

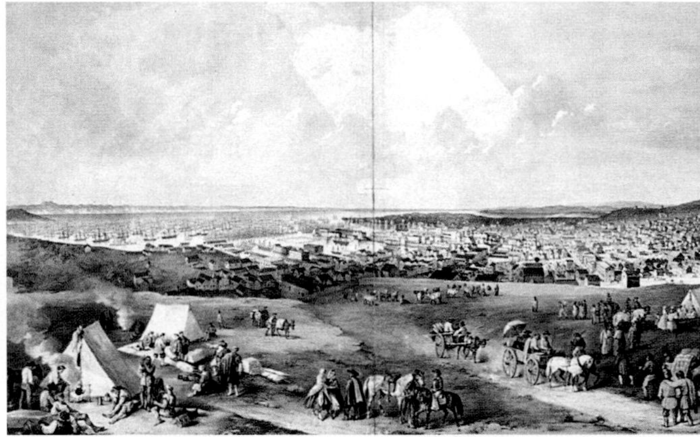

ABOVE: By the early 1850s San Francisco was a riotous boom town and the center of the Gold Rush. The forest of ship masts in the bay stand testament to the hordes of prospectors who made their way to the interior through the port, many of whom could not afford to stay at San Francisco's new hotels and camped on the town's outskirts instead.

locals might think of today's California as a state of kooks, movie moguls, and beach bums, they couldn't be more wrong. In truth, the culture of California perfectly mirrors its scenery. This is a place of diversity and of extremes. California is an amazing amalgam, a gloriously diverse profusion, a place where cultures haven't so much collided as mingled, and in doing so created something unique and almost mythical.

Today, California generates more wealth than any other state (if it were a separate country it would rank as about the ninth richest in the world), and it has achieved this in an impressively short amount of time. The state owes some of its success to its natural bounty, of course, but a lot more to the people who have made their homes here and who, over the years, have transformed California from virtual wilderness to wonderland.

The Golden State adopted its official nickname in 1968 and, as nicknames go, it is particularly appropriate. When gold was discovered in the state in 1848, it sparked an explosion. At the time the entire state had a non-native population of

LEFT: News of the Gold Rush reached every corner of the globe, including China, which at that time was considerably easier to reach across the Pacific than the East Coast of the United States was by either sea or land. Many Chinese made the journey, and while some dispersed across the landscape, others remained in San Francisco to found the city's famous Chinatown district.

only 15,000 (in comparison, New York City alone was then home to over half a million people). But gold brought men, women, and their children to the state to make their fortunes from every corner of the United States and beyond. In that first great Gold Rush some 300,000 "forty-niners" swamped California, and while a few struck it rich, all of them found gold of a different kind: meadows carpeted with golden poppies each spring and bathed in a honeyed golden sunlight. They found a place not just rich in gold, but with natural ports, fertile valleys, and abundant resources of every kind. Word soon leaked out. The following decades would see ever more people arrive—by 1900, over 1.2 million, a number which almost doubled over the following decade and kept accelerating. These days California is home to some thirty-seven million people.

Before the arrival of gold hunters, the region had been home to hundreds of Native American tribes, some of whose descendants still dwell in the area. The first European to visit was Juan Rodrigues Cabrillo, a Portuguese explorer who sailed up the coast in 1542. The name of the state—which originally also encompassed areas of Nevada, Utah, Arizona, Wyoming, and the Mexican peninsula of Baja California—is popularly believed to derive from the fabled Amazonian Queen Califia, who ruled over a faraway paradise rich in gold. If so, it was an extraordinarily appropriate name to pick, as residents and visitors to the golden state agree.

Despite a visit from the illustrious British navigator Sir Francis Drake in 1579 and subsequent feuding over the region by the two maritime superpowers, the region's early history belonged to Spain, bequeathing California a Latin heritage that is evident to this day. In 1769, the first of twenty-one Franciscan missions opened at San Diego (Mission San Diego de Alcala also introduced wine making to the region along with other European fruits and vegetables). The monks, led by Fr. Junipero Serra, attempted to convert the local inhabitants with

RIGHT: In 1864, Yosemite became the first instance of land being specifically set aside for preservation and public use, and by the 1870s tourists newly arrived on the Transcontinental Railroad could take a special stagecoach to visit the park. It was sill a relatively arduous journey, but scenes like this one of Yosemite Valley from Glacier Point were well worth the effort.

RIGHT: By the end of the nineteenth century, California had a thriving tourist industry and lavish hotels, such as the Moorish-influenced Hotel Green in Pasadena, which opened in 1899, were becoming commonplace throughout the state. The famous old hotel has welcomed many famous names over the years, including numerous U.S. presidents, and continues to offer guests a taste of days past.

LEFT: California's citrus fruit industry dates back to the 1870s in Riverside, when Eliza Tibbets received two trees as a gift from a friend at the Department of Agriculture in Washington, D.C. Those first two orange trees thrived under the California sunshine. A few years later, full scale farming was underway.

ABOVE: San Francisco at the turn of the century was a successful, bustling city that had to some extent put its bawdy reputation of the Gold Rush years behind it. Under the auspices of mayor James D. Phelan, who was elected in 1896, new sewers, schools, parks, and a hospital were built. It would be Phelan's personal crusade to make San Francisco into the "Paris of the West." The city still faced some hard times though. In 1901, the year this photograph was taken, a ship brought rats infected with bubonic plague to the city, and it was not until 1905 that the disease was completely eradicated.

ABOVE: California's first incorporated city (in 1850), San Jose served as the state's capital from 1849 to 1852. By 1907 it was a prosperous, if rather sleepy, farming community.

mixed success, but also provided a firm Spanish foothold in the region. Soon they were joined by countrymen and -women lured to the New World by the offer of large land grants. Normally these were used to raise sheep and cattle, and the Spanish pioneers began the age of the California ranchos. It is interesting to note that even in those days African-Americans were present in California, farming and running businesses. Although their number swelled significantly during the early twentieth century, black Californians were among the state's early settlers.

By 1821, California was part of the newly independent Mexico and welcoming more new arrivals. The trappers and pioneers of the United States who braved the long, hard trails across the continent have been eulogized in film and fiction, but less well known is that Russia also started a small settlement and trading post at Fort Ross around this time, adding a little more flavor to California's cultural soup. Despite the area's undoubted natural advantages, the overland Siskiyou, California, and Oregon Trails made for a long and dangerous crossing of an entire continent over mountain ranges and deserts in wagons and the five-month (or more) voyage by sea around Cape Horn was just as perilous. Passengers would endure terrifying storms, extreme temperatures, disease, and turbulent waters. Unsurprisingly, it was a journey that few undertook.

For a short time (1846–1847), the state overthrew Mexican rule and became independent, though it was quickly occu-

RIGHT: For many tourists back in the 1930s, as now, California's great attraction was Hollywood. Hollywood Boulevard was often bathed in searchlights for the premiere of a new movie or a celebrity event, and visitors flocked to breathe the same air as their idols and soak up the atmosphere in the City of Dreams.

ABOVE: By the 1940s Los Angeles had a population of over a million people, drawn to the city by the motion picture and aviation industries, and the affluent city was growing increasingly gentrified. Wilshire Boulevard had become one of the principal thoroughfares, lined with businesses, hotels, and shops, such as Bullocks Wilshire department store, the tower of which can be seen on the left of the photograph.

OPPOSITE, TOP: More than any other band, the Beach Boys—pictured here playing at the Hollywood Bowl in 1965—captured the sights and sounds of California in the Sixties. Songs like "Fun Fun Fun" and "I Get Around" perfectly summed up the carefree teenage lifestyle. You could hear the sunshine in every note.

LEFT: The Fifties and Sixties were great days to be young in California. Postwar baby boomers came of age in a state that was richer than ever and rock 'n' roll was in full swing. Popularized by songs such as "California Girls" and "Do You Know the Way to San Jose?," California was widely seen as a beach paradise. Natives were joined in their partying by youngsters from all over the country who preferred a low-paying job and a shack on the beach in California to a career back home.

BELOW: San Francisco in 1967 was the epicenter of the Summer of Love. As many as 100,000 people, including George Harrison of the Beatles, swamped the Haight-Ashbury district of San Francisco to join in the political, sexual, and creative revolution.

pied by the United States early in the Mexican-American War. The California Republic's first and only president was deposed after governing for just twenty-five days. In 1848—the same year the war ended—gold was discovered at Sutter's Mill in Coloma and the eyes of the world turned to the previously obscure state. In the immediate aftermath the port of San Francisco was packed with boats whose entire crews had deserted in the race to find gold, and they were not alone. Hundreds of thousands made the perilous journey, and though almost all of them were fixated on making a fortune rather than settling down, many were seduced by California's beauty and its possibilities and never made it back east. The effects of the Gold Rush were startling. Small villages such as San Francisco swelled into boomtowns almost overnight. Roads were built and fields plowed, while churches, schools, and completely new towns were also hastily erected. Word of the wealth that waited in California swept the world: Now the state also saw its first arrivals from China.

The completion of the First Transcontinental Railroad in 1869 made

California easier to reach and spawned a fresh wave of migration from the eastern United States. Among the newcomers were recent immigrants from every corner of Europe. With the arrival of highways in the early twentieth century, the flood became a deluge. By 1965 California was the most populous state in the Union, and the most diverse. These days, California's population includes people who can trace their ancestry to just about every nation on Earth. Some are new arrivals, attracted to the opportunities offered by the Golden State, while others can trace their California heritage back through generations. With so many

RIGHT: It wasn't only the teenagers who flocked to the state to relax. Families enjoyed the sunshine at new low-cost motels like this one on the beach at Monterey.

different peoples being brought together over such a relatively short period, there have—unfortunately—been tensions over the years, but on the whole such close association has fostered a relaxed, accommodating California temper that perhaps takes something from the best of all the peoples who have made their lives here. Something of the attitude of the early pioneers still exists here, too. California is a state where if you can imagine it, you can do it. With a little application and know-how, anything is possible.

This book offers glimpses back at some of the days and the lives that have shaped the state. Some will be familiar. Who could resist including some Hollywood glitz and San Francisco's Painted Ladies, for example? Other images are less often seen. From simple family life to the great engineering feats that helped build the state, these are no less important parts of the state's heritage. Still other images show the quirky, warm side of California. With such incredible riches to offer, no single volume could hope to do more than scratch the surface of how this remarkable place came to be, but we hope to have captured something of its individuality within these pages. This is the way we were in California.

THE SAN FRANCISCO EARTHQUAKE 1906

Blessed in so many ways, California also faces ever-present danger from nature. The San Andreas Fault runs the entire length of the state and earthquakes are regular occurrences. None has been so devastating as that of April 18, 1906. The northern third of the fault ruptured in a shock that lasted forty-two seconds and caused damage as far south as San Jose. San Francisco was virtually destroyed in

BELOW: Shocked San Franciscans stare down Sacramento Street while their ruined city burns.

LEFT AND BELOW: Many of those houses that survived the quake, the aftershocks, and the devastating fire were nevertheless tumbled from their foundations.

the quake and the fire that followed. While only 376 deaths were reported at the time, the final toll rose to over 3,000 and about three quarters of the city's inhabitants were left homeless. Nevertheless, with characteristic grit and determination the people of San Francisco rebuilt at an astounding pace, making their city stronger and more beautiful than before. By 1915, San Francisco had risen from the ashes in time for the celebratory Panama-Pacific Exposition.

ABOVE: With admirable spirit some citizens took the destruction of their homes and livelihoods with a pinch of humor. The "House of Mirth" became San Francisco's most famous upscale hotel after the quake.

LEFT: San Francisco reduced to rubble. Over 80 percent of the city was destroyed as this image from a damaged glass-plate negative shows.

MAJOR ATTRACTIONS

Tens of millions of visitors a year and a still increasing population attest to the fact that California is one big attraction. This is a place that has everything: a year-round warm, sunny climate, exciting cities and picturesque villages, incredible vistas, national parks, theme parks, museums, and historic sites. And that's just the beginning. Here you can swim in the Pacific Ocean in the morning and ski in the Sierra Nevada by afternoon, drive historic Route 101 and catch the spectacular views at Big Sur, or soak up cinema history on the Hollywood Walk of Fame. In the south of the state are palm-fringed sandy beaches, and to the north rugged hiking trails and secluded beaches from where it's possible to observe seals, sea otters, and whales at play. Inland are world famous vineyards, the stunning waterfalls of Yosemite National Park, towns such as Bakersfield steeped in American culture, and atmospheric ghost towns, reminders of California's roots. The list of wonders goes on and on. From incredible engineering feats such as the Golden Gate Bridge to folksy antique and bric-a-brac markets, from the picturesque winding cable cars of San Francisco and the historic Spanish missions of San Diego to jaw-dropping roller coasters, California has something to please everyone.

"Big Sur is the California that men dreamed of years ago, this is the Pacific that Balboa looked at from the Peak of Darien, this is the face of the earth as the Creator intended it to look."

Henry Miller

ABOVE: This 1934 tourist poster managed to work many of California's charms into a single image: stunning scenery, sunshine, the ocean, picturesque towns, and outdoor adventure.

Today the attractions of California are famous throughout the world, but as recently as 1848 the region was largely

ABOVE: Tourists take their ease on Eagle Peak in Yosemite, 1902.

LEFT: Mariposa Grove, near Wawona at the south of Yosemite National Park, has been popular with tourists since the mid-nineteenth century. The large hole at the base of the "Wawona Tree" was cut in 1881 to allow tourists to drive through, though sadly this weakened the tree and it fell in 1969 under the weight of snow in its branches.

ignored by all save the most adventurous. California was truly the "Wild West." While hundreds of thousands arrived to find their fortune in the Gold Rush of '49, few then thought of the state's attractions outside of the wealth that could be found beneath its hills and in the riverbeds. This, however, soon changed. When the railway arrived in 1869, it did not take long for businesses to capitalize on California's charms. At the time, California was seen as an exotic novelty, an untamed wilderness of natural magnificence that was also now easier to reach. By 1870, the first posters advertising the state to tourists went up in New York, and curious travelers eagerly took up the offer of a trip that could now be completed in around eighty-four hours rather than four months. They came in droves and found in California the same attractions as subsequent generations: astounding scenery that would have been almost completely

RIGHT: The delightful Santa Catalina Island was developed as a tourist resort at the end of the nineteenth century and enjoyed immediate success. The island was served by a regular steamer, and at the little settlement of Avalon, visitors could enjoy the facilities of the Hotel Metropole, a pier, and a dance pavilion, while the men were welcome to gamble at the Pilgrim Club.

ABOVE AND RIGHT: In 1915 San Diego became the smallest city ever to have staged a World's Fair, but despite the city's relatively small population of about 40,000 and competition from a similar San Francisco event that opened the same year, the exposition in Balboa Park held to celebrate the opening of the Panama Canal was phenomenally successful. The grounds welcomed four million people from all over the world and bequeathed the city some of its most beloved landmarks such as the California Building and the Balboa Park Botanical Garden (right).

alien to those who had spent their lives in the East, the glittering Pacific Ocean, and cities brimming with excitement.

For people coming to find their fortunes, the attraction of California lay in the myriad new business opportunities that were springing up there. Not least among these was the movie industry. The first Hollywood film—*In Old California*—was shot in the small village found by director D. W. Griffith in 1910, and just five years later most of the nation's new movies were being made in Hollywood. Hordes of would-be actors and actresses made the pilgrimage then, as they do today.

With economic success came attractions of a different kind. California began building pleasure parks, botanical gardens, and sports grounds. In 1853, just three years after joining the Union, San Francisco had its first museum. Today, the California Academy of Natural Sciences is one of the biggest natural history museums in the world. Work also started on Golden Gate Park in 1875, giving the city a magnificent outdoor space that would host a World's Fair in 1894. Balboa Park in San Diego also dates to this heady time. In 1915 the park also hosted a World's Fair (the Panama-California Exposition), in the same year that San Francisco hosted the Panama-Pacific Exposition to celebrate the reconstruction of the city after the 1906 earthquake. Millions came to see the showcases. A few years later another of the state's great cities—Los Angeles—played host to the 1932 Summer Olympic Games at the Los Angeles Memorial Coliseum (which, in

1984, became the only venue ever to have hosted two Olympics).

As the century progressed and more and more people arrived, Californians surpassed themselves in offering new and exciting ways for tourists and locals alike to enjoy themselves. As the center of the movie industry, Los Angeles contributed spectacular movie palaces such as Grauman's Chinese Theatre (1927), while from 1939 audiences thousands strong could attend concerts outdoors at the Hollywood Bowl. In 1955, California also gave children around the world a new adventure to dream of when it opened Disneyland in Anaheim. The theme park template has since been copied around the world, but Disneyland still reigns supreme. Since its opening day well over 500 million visitors have passed through the turnstiles.

But the state wasn't just developing parks, museums, and tourist attractions. Distinct cultures were also budding here and these had an allure all their own. By the Fifties surf life was entering the mainstream, popularized by movies such as *Gidget* (1959) and bands like The Beach Boys. In response, young people flocked to take part in the laid-back sun and fun

LEFT AND BELOW: The centerpiece of San Francisco's Panama-Pacific Exposition, which ran from February to December, 1915, was the Tower of Jewels, which was studded with more than 100,000 glass "gems" that glittered during the day and sparkled under the light of fifty search-lights at night. Other attractions were Festival Hall, the California Building, and the Palace of Fine Arts (below left), which remains a much loved part of San Francisco's cityscape and is now popular as a wedding venue.

style. Farther north, San Francisco became the spiritual home of the "Beat Generation" around the same time, and in the next decade its Haight-Ashbury district was the epicenter of hippie culture. Around the world California became synonymous with youth and freedom. Perhaps this is California's most enduring attraction. Whatever your age, this is a state where it's easy to feel as if anything is possible. Built by pioneers and visionaries, all around is evidence that California is a place that prizes the imagination and dreams of the future.

LEFT: Star spotters and young actors made regular pilgrimages to Hollywood's Brown Derby restaurant, which counted the movie stars of the day among its clientele.

RIGHT: Not every eager young actress was from out of town. Norma Jean Baker was born in Los Angeles County Hospital and the local girl would later become the most glamorous of Hollywood's stars under her adopted name Marilyn Monroe.

DISNEYLAND

The brainchild of Walt Disney and the only one of the Disney parks to be personally designed by the great man, Disneyland opened in Anaheim on July 17, 1955, and was the first of its kind anywhere in the world. Famously, the opening day did not go well: It was an unusually hot day and a plumbers' strike meant that water fountains were not working, while a gas leak closed down Fantasyland, Adventureland, and Frontierland. The park was soon operating smoothly though, and the fifteen million customers that now visit annually are a testament to Disney's enduring genius.

RIGHT: Opening day was by invitation only, and though forged tickets were another of the opening day problems, there were many celebrities among the crowds who rushed to enjoy the Disney magic in Sleeping Beauty's Castle.

LEFT: This young man may have been the first—though by no means the last—child to have lost his parents at Disneyland. Fortunately, the Disney police force were there to help.

LEFT: Disney designed the park to offer fun to everyone, as Sisters Mary William and Mary Alfred found out during a Catholic school day out in 1962.

BOOKS

LEFT: California attracted intellectuals as well as vacationers. One of the most famous gathering places for poets and writers was San Francisco's City Lights Bookstore (a historic landmark since 2001 and still in operation today). Founded by Lawrence Ferlinghetti in 1953, the store became notorious during a 1956 obscenity trial after it published Allen Ginsberg's (seen here at the center of the group) *Howl and Other Poems*.

ABOVE: Californians' love of beach life has remained undiminished since the earliest days of the state. Over the years, uncountable memories have been made by the Pacific, from fire-lit late-night barbecues and parties to days under the sun playing volleyball or relaxing with friends and family.

RIGHT: The fabulous sunken gardens, exhibit palaces, and exposition tower of the Golden Gate International Exposition, which was held on Treasure Island in San Francisco Bay from February to December, 1939. Celebrating the completion of the San Francisco–Oakland Bay Bridge and the Golden Gate Bridge, the fair featured a mile-long esplanade ornamented with sculptures by California artists as well as a profusion of local flowers and an eighty-foot statue, *Pacifica*, which symbolized unity between the Pacific nations.

RIGHT: As well as showcasing California's architectural and natural delights, the Golden Gate International Exposition of 1939 had an amusement zone called "The Gayway," which offered less cerebral entertainment. Visitors could see 1939 Miss America Patricia Donnelly in the flesh or visit the Daydreams Girl Show. One of the zone's most popular draws was Sally Rand's Nude Ranch.

RIGHT: An artist's paradise, California has attracted some of the world's most illustrious painters. Salvador Dali and his wife Gala visited in 1941 and the surrealist made sketches throughout his visit, including one of this Monterey Cypress tree at Del Monte.

ABOVE AND RIGHT: At sunrise near Mount Whitney, California's tallest peak, the dark scrubland is transformed into a breathtaking sci-fi landscape of oranges, blues, and purples.

RIGHT: The Lone Pine area is fascinating for its natural rugged beauty and its role in film history. It's been used as an important source of location footage since the 1920s. Although countless westerns were filmed there, it's also been used to depict the Sahara Desert (as here with Errol Flynn and David Niven in *The Charge of the Light Brigade*), the Himalayas, and even the terrain of other planets.

LEFT: Alcatraz Island—also known as the Rock—shut down as a penitentiary in 1963, having held some of America's most notorious criminals over its twenty-nine-year history as a prison. Its tough reputation, mythical escape attempts (no prisoner ever successfully escaped), and place in popular culture ensured that even before guided tours were available plenty of people wanted to observe the jail from a distance.

RIGHT: By the Forties Palm Springs was a fashionable and laid-back resort and much frequented by the Hollywood glitterati. Vacationers could avail themselves of golf, tennis, horseback riding, or hiking in the desert, or just let it all hang out and enjoy some light shopping.

KHOURY'S CAFE
DRINK
Coca-Cola
LEO'S
SERVICE
Malts 25¢
LEO'S PLACE
ROYAL CROWN
COLA
BEST BY TASTE-TEST
CONE
CANDIED APPLE
COTTON CANDY
10¢

OPPOSITE AND LEFT: The sight of bodybuilders on the beach has been familiar to Californians since the 1930s. The original Muscle Beach was at Santa Monica and became incredibly popular with tourists who came to see the tricks and stunts of circus performers and strongmen. By 1959, Santa Monica couldn't cope with the growing crowds any longer, and Muscle Beach was moved to Venice, where it has long been a favorite of bodybuilders including Governor Arnold Schwarzenegger, who worked out there regularly in the 1970s.

MAKING A STATE

In California it is possible to lose yourself in the wilderness, or to drive dusty roads through the desert for hours on end without seeing so much as another car. Anyone who wishes to look can still find the state's wild history. Yet, despite this, California is the most advanced of American states. For one that's on the very edge of the continent and a relative latecomer to industry or development of any kind, that's quite an achievement. But as the nineteenth-century financial analyst John Moody was quick to recognize, California is rich in natural resources and opportunity. From the earliest days of the Gold Rush, its people—civic leaders, business tycoons, and ordinary folk—have all conspired to prove him right and build a state where the possibilities are still almost unlimited. These days, California is crisscrossed with roads and connected to the world by state-of-the-art international airports and technology pioneered right inside its borders. Historically powered by oil from its extensive oil fields, it is now one of the greenest

People began to understand that with the acquisition of California the nation had obtained practically half a continent, of which the future possibilities were almost unlimited, so far as the development of natural resources and the general production of wealth were concerned.

John Moody

RIGHT: A familiar scene across California's gold fields by 1850—seen here on the Daley Claim in Columbia, Tuolumne County—were the hoisting wheels that lifted rock out of newly dug mine shafts.

LEFT: The tiny Sutter's Mill, photographed in 1850, was responsible for a dramatic change in California's fortunes. When Sutter's partner James Marshall found a few flakes of gold here in 1848, he and Sutter tried to keep it secret, but it wasn't long before word spread. By the following year tens of thousands of "Forty-Niners" were rushing to the state from the east and further abroad to share in the bounty.

states, actively pursuing renewable energy sources such as hydroelectric, solar, geothermic, and wind power. Its schools, protected by a unique amendment to the constitution, guarantee a minimum level of funding per pupil, while California State University is the largest in the United States and also employs more Nobel Prize winners than any other university system in the world. In the California State Water Project, it has the largest public water system in the world. Nowadays, as you might expect in a state whose population continues to grow year after year, there is

ABOVE: Within a decade of the Transcontinental Railroad being finished, tracks had spread across California allowing the development of a busy tourist industry. The Henry M. Stanley party was headed for Monterey when this photograph was taken in 1891.

ABOVE: One of the greatest problems faced by Californians in the years after the Gold Rush was a lack of water, particularly in the southern parts of the state where low rainfall meant frequent shortages. One solution was to bring water down from the Sierra Nevada, as was adopted for the Los Angeles Aqueduct, while another was the construction of dams across rivers to keep spring runoff from melting snow in reserve for the dry summer months. The Sweetwater Dam in San Diego was completed in 1888 and was at the time the biggest of its kind in the country.

LEFT: Edward Doheny and Charles Canfield's discovery of oil in Los Angeles in 1892 heralded the "black gold rush." Within a few years, hundreds of wells across the state were pumping out millions of barrels each year, bringing even more wealth to California.

inevitable fretting that the infrastructure of the future will not be able to cope, but with the aplomb of their forebears, Californians will doubtless renew, expand, and reinvent where necessary to keep their state on the cutting edge.

The first great challenge for new Californians in the mid-nineteenth century was distance and the landscape of continental North America. As noted in the previous chapters, reaching the state was prohibitively difficult and could often be fatal. Relief of sorts came with the Panama Railway in 1855, which meant that steamships could now drop passengers on the eastern side of the Panama Isthmus from where they could take a day's journey by train (rather than a week in canoes through the jungle) to the west and then another ship northward. At a stroke this cut months off the trip (and incidentally provided a safer route for gold traveling eastward). Yet it was still a lengthy and expensive journey. Accordingly, most gold seekers took the overland trails, usually the California Trail, and faced the dangers of inhospitable terrain and attack from hostile Native American tribes instead.

The answer to this, and to other

RIGHT AND OPPOSITE: The Rancho La Brea Tarpits, in Hancock Park. For many years children have been fascinated by the woolly mammoth statue drowning in a great pool of tar. Even before the George C. Page Museum was built, field trips brought elementary school classes to see the bubbling liquid, smell the tar, and watch archaeologists cleaning fossils at the active pits. The beautifully designed museum was opened in 1977 and holds the largest collection of Ice Age plants and animals in the world. George C. Page typifies the California ideal. As a teenager he came to the state with nothing because he loved the taste of oranges and wanted to see the place they came from. He started by selling fruit and later founded the Mission Pak company, which distributed California produce to the rest of the country. He used his vast fortune to give back to the state of California. Located right next to the Los Angeles County Museum of Art, the Hancock Park area is still a favorite outing in Los Angeles.

problems (including the threat of secession in California), was to connect to the United States' new western outpost to the east using the modern and quick medium of the railway. When the first stage of the line was complete, it stretched from Omaha to Sacramento and, for the first time, made it easy to travel from one side of the United States to the other. But the story of the railway in California didn't stop there. Within a few months, the line had been extended to the coast at Oakland, and within a year the completion of the Denver Pacific Line in Colorado heralded the first truly coast-to-coast services. Meanwhile an iron web of lines spread across the state, connecting older settlements and leaving in its wake bustling new towns and farms. California would grow in population, wealth, and political importance at an unheard-of rate. The West had been won.

Another surprise lay beneath the earth in California. In 1892 two mineral prospectors who happened to be in downtown Los Angeles spotted tar on the wheels of their cart. Edward Doheny and Charles Canfield quickly mounted a

TOP LEFT AND MIDDLE LEFT: California has a distinguished heritage of viniculture that dates back to the eighteenth century. The industry suffered a devastating setback in the late nineteenth century when the phylloxera epidemic destroyed entire vineyards and another when Prohibition put all but 140 out of business. The few that survived scraped through the lean years making sacramental wine and nonalcoholic grape juice, and soon after the Eighteenth Amendment was repealed, wine making was booming again.

BOTTOM LEFT AND RIGHT: San Francisco's famous cable cars date back to 1872 when the Clay Street line began running the first services and over the years became an integral part of the cityscape. Although the system was largely replaced by electric streetcars after the 1906 earthquake (as seen at right running along the newly rebuilt Market Street), the city refused to give up its beloved cable cars, and today San Francisco's are the only remaining examples still in use anywhere in the world.

drilling operation (they are said to have used a sharpened eucalyptus tree as a drill) and, at roughly 450 feet, struck oil. Even more people flocked to the state to take part in the bonanza.

By the turn of the twentieth century, California had a population of almost 1.5 million, most of whom lived in burgeoning inland towns like Stockton (incorporated 1850) and Bakersfield (incorporated 1869) and the old coastal cities of San Francisco, San Jose, Los Angeles, and San Diego. Supplying the basic needs of these new inhabitants was of vital importance, and the state responded with typically audacious solutions. Engineering projects such as the 1910 Los Angeles Aqueduct, which brought clean water 223 miles through the Mojave Desert to dry Los Angeles, were followed by massive dams such as the Hetch Hetchy (finished in 1923), which still supplies San Francisco with water and electricity. In 1913 the state also welcomed the Lincoln Highway, which created a direct road link from Times Square in New York City to Lincoln Park in San Francisco. Driving would become Californians' favorite form of transport over the following decades, leading to the famous traffic jams in and

LEFT: Today Long Beach is the sixth largest city in California, but it began its history as the site of two adjoining ranchos that became a small farming community toward the end of the nineteenth century. As the influx of tourists into California grew, Long Beach was developed into a resort town and was extremely popular from about 1902 onward, when it earned the nickname "Little Iowa" for all the Midwesterners who vacationed there.

ABOVE: Tourism also plays a large role in the history of Redondo Beach. Originally the Rancho San Pedro, it was once the first port of Los Angeles. Like Long Beach, the small community here became popular with visitors, not least because of its wide sands and the acres of flowers at Carnation Gardens. Soon hotels such as the luxurious Hotel Redondo with its eighteen-hole golf course and tennis courts were catering to the well-to-do, while those with less money to spend could camp out at Tent City.

BELOW: Another former rancho, by 1908 the city of Redlands in San Bernardino County was so beautiful that the Santa Fe Railroad put on special excursion trains for tourists to take in the city's orange groves and rose-planted streets.

around the state's major cities. Notwithstanding the frustration of the commuters of the future, at the time the expanding road system was another major boost to tourism and immigration.

As the twentieth century progressed, new fortunes were made in property development and industry as airplane manufacturers and military shipyards set up shop in the state. The combination of wealth flowing into the public coffers and wise civic planning, including the adoption of an education system that has become the envy of the world, set the scene for the information technology revolution of the latter half of the century. "Silicon Valley" outside San Francisco become the center of the new high-tech industries just as Hollywood continued to be the center of the movie industry.

In many other respects California has been a world leader: in public services such as hospitals, police, and fire departments, as well as in air transport and provision of parks and sports grounds. The state may have been a late starter, but it has swiftly caught up with areas of the world that had a head start of centuries and in many ways surpassed them. And it shows no signs of slowing down. Moody's early assessment of California as a state where the possibilities are "almost unlimited" is as true now as it was 150 years ago.

LEFT: With its long Pacific coast, access to the Atlantic via the Panama Canal, and excellent ports, California was an obvious choice as a hub for the Navy and the shipbuilding industry. During wartime the state was of vital importance to the war effort, and again, the population rose dramatically. The Richmond Shipyards were the most prolific of California's World War II shipbuilding sites. Laborers, including men and women from all over the country, swelled the city's population from 20,000 to 100,000 and launched about 750 vessels during the conflict. Among them was the *Robert E. Perry*, which took just eleven days to build and fit and was launched on November 12, 1942.

ABOVE AND LEFT: The aviation industry is important to California and has been for many years. North American Aviation Inc. built large numbers of P-51s and B-25s (above) during World War II and the iconic F-86 Sabre after the war. The XB-70 Valkyrie bomber (left) was a huge project in El Segundo throughout the 1960s. Despite the development costs and a flight speed three times that of sound, the 275-ton XB-70 didn't make it into service. By then experts thought rocket warfare had made continental bombers obsolete, and many engineers moved from the Valkyrie to the space shuttle.

RIGHT, TOP: The aviation industry found an early home in California, where clear blue skies were perfect for testing and training. Douglas Aircraft opened its headquarters at Long Beach in 1921, while magnate and adventurer Howard Hughes founded Hughes Aircraft at Glendale in 1932. But the first California-based company was Lockheed, which started in Santa Barbara in 1912 and moved to Hollywood in 1926. In 1930 Lockheed also made this special "Sirius" plane for aviator Charles Lindbergh and his wife.

RIGHT: The heat-scorched Apollo 13 command module was built at the North American Rockwell plant. It was returned after being plucked from the Pacific so that engineers and scientists could examine it to determine what went wrong with the mission.

RIGHT: Rows of parked cars in the California desert near Edwards Air Force Base. Visitors from throughout the United States gathered to watch the space shuttle landing on the morning of July 4, 1982.

OPPOSITE, BOTTOM RIGHT: The space shuttle *Challenger* crawls through the streets of Palmdale.

THE TRANSCONTINENTAL RAILROAD

The building of the Transcontinental Railroad was an important turning point in California's development. In 1862, President Abraham Lincoln signed the Pacific Railway Act into law, and seven years later, on May 10, 1869, the "Golden Spike" was driven into the track by Governor Leland Stanford at Promontory Summit, Utah, where the lines from east and west joined. The country erupted in celebration. The completion of the First Transcontinental Railroad is rightly considered one of the great engineering feats of the nineteenth century.

RIGHT: To the east the Union Pacific Railroad laid 1,087 miles of track westward from the Council Bluffs, Iowa/Omaha area using primarily Irish labor. In the west the Central Pacific Railroad, using work gangs that included large numbers of Chinese immigrants, worked eastward for 690 miles from Sacramento over the Sierra Nevada.

ABOVE: Chinese laborers worked in sometimes difficult conditions including fierce heat and heavy snow with picks, shovels, and wheelbarrows.

LEFT: As the rails spread across California, tiny stations like the Feather River Inn Depot sprang up as depots for timber and farm products. Settlers congregated around the stations, and some of these small communities gradually grew into full-fledged towns.

TOP RIGHT: By the 1920s Californians had turned their backs on rail travel and adopted the motor car instead. With the arrival of the Lincoln Highway in 1913 and the spread of roads across the state came new innovations such as The Stein, one of the first drive-through beer and rest stops.

FAR RIGHT: The "drive-through" idea was an immediate hit in California, and by the middle of the twentieth century citizens could enjoy drive-in movies, drive-through restaurants, and even drive-up auto-banks.

BOTTOM RIGHT: Bumper-to-bumper traffic on California's highways is nothing new. By 1954 car-loving Californians were swamping the state's roads, and back-ups on major arteries such as the Arroyo Seco Freeway were frequent.

AUTO BANKING
SIDEWALK TELLER WINDOW
4R1 49Z

RIGHT: Probably the most famous suspension bridge in the world, San Francisco's Golden Gate Bridge, was the longest of its kind on its completion in 1937. Connecting the San Francisco Peninsula to Marin County, it was painted with red lead primer and a matching topcoat to give it its distinctive color and quickly became one of the state's best-loved landmarks as well as a tourist attraction in its own right.

ABOVE: Clear sunlight and dramatic locations made California an ideal spot for the fledgling movie industry to set up shop. By the 1930s hundreds of films were being made annually on sets in Hollywood and on location—here at Laguna Beach.

RIGHT: Best remembered for the slapstick Keystone Cops, the Keystone movie studios were also famous at the time for their "bathing beauties" films. These made good use of two resources that never ran short in California: hopeful starlets and sunny beaches.

RIGHT: The Farmers' Market at Third and Fairfax. This collection of restaurants, food stalls, and shops was originally built in the 1930s. Adjacent to the CBS studios, it was a favorite place for movie and TV stars' lunch breaks. Today the outskirts of the market have been replaced by a modern shopping center, but the original stalls and structures at the heart of the market remain unchanged, with the same pale green metal folding chairs and tables scattered throughout. Bob's Donuts still makes the best doughnuts in Los Angeles and continues to receive awards to prove it.

CALIFORNIA AT HOME

"Craziness" may be too strong a word, but it's certainly true that Californians have embraced the gamut of architectural styles over the years. Today, their homes are as wonderfully diverse as the landscape they occupy and the people who live in them. You'll find historic adobe houses of the early Spanish colonists, swanky Hollywood mansions, the delightful Victorian "Painted Ladies" of San Francisco, a precious handful of "California Textile Block" houses created specifically for the state by America's most illustrious architect—Frank Lloyd Wright, neoclassical houses with carefully landscaped gardens, and everything in between. Whether they chose an extravagant palace such as Hearst Castle in the hills above San Simeon, a Mediterranean-influenced casa, or a sleek, modernist condominium, the people who have lived here have stamped their homes with a bewildering range of styles, many of which have become so associated with the state that they are now unmistakably Californian.

"California lacks a lot of the rules and restrictions the East has. Every house is a different style, different material, different color. There's a lot of craziness out there."

Parker Stevenson

ABOVE: Laguna Beach in 1914 was a struggling shorefront village that earned extra money by renting houses to farmers who came there to escape the summer heat. During the following decade the picturesque community of simple clapboard houses became a haven for visiting artists who founded the creative community that is found in the town to this day.

OPPOSITE: The main house of the Keystone Farm in Kern County was typical of rural California domestic architecture. Constructed simply from timber, most houses borrowed from the tradition of pueblo design and had a veranda where families could cool down in the shade.

LEFT: In wealthy San Francisco homes were more ornate and built in the fashionable style of the Victorian era. As far back as 1849, it was all the rage to paint the façade in daring colors, leading a sniffy journalist to write in 1885, "Red, yellow, chocolate, orange, everything that is loud is in fashion...if the upper stories are not of red or blue...they are painted up into uncouth panels of yellow and brown...." The practice fell out of style in the early twentieth century, following the 1906 earthquake, but was revived by a San Francisco artist in the early Sixties and soon caught on again. The popular nickname of the city's "Painted Ladies" was coined by writers Elizabeth Pomada and Michael Larsen for their 1978 book, *Painted Ladies: San Francisco's Resplendent Victorians*.

Away from the Spanish presidio forts, the first non-native "homes" in California were the missions. The pueblo-style adobe architecture has been revived many times over the years and is still much in evidence today. No two of the twenty-one California missions are quite the same, but all reflect the style of the Spanish homeland. (The Mission San Luis Rey de Francia, in what is now Oceanside, is notable in also introducing a few Moorish features to California architecture.) Over the following decades of the nineteenth century Spain, and later Mexico, began granting tens of thousands of acres in land parcels to prospective settlers. The new cattle ranchers of California styled themselves after the great landholders of Spain, and as they became established—and some became wealthy—their home life reflected their new status. The typical ranch house will be familiar to anyone who has watched an old Western movie. Taking their design from the same pueblo style as the missions, they were adobe buildings, usually with a shaded veranda. Much of the work on the ranch was done by Native American labor, giving the landowners a relatively luxurious lifestyle. Visits to neighboring ranches were popular and a chance for rowdy fiestas, with the menfolk showing off their equestrian skills in rodeos.

Although they would leave a lasting impact on California in the division of lands, the great age of the rancheros came to an end with the Gold Rush of 1849 and California's entry into the United States. Now California witnessed tens of thousands of new arrivals, and for the vast majority homes and settlements had to be built from scratch, though it is interesting to note that some of the world's first self-assembly kit homes were also used. For a taste of how the early miners lived, it is still possible to visit the towns that once hummed with industry but now stand empty. The old silver-mining ghost town of Calico, for example, gives an evocative sense of life in the Old West, down to its cemetery overlooking the Mojave Desert. Now a tourist attraction, at its peak Calico was a town of some 1,200 souls and had the usual complement of churches, bars, brothels, and—more unusually—its own newspaper. Although most of the homes there have been re-created from old photographs, it's possible to sense how those pioneering Californians must have lived beneath the desert sun in cramped quarters.

RIGHT: By the end of the nineteenth century, the homes of the newly wealthy Californians were becoming increasingly ornate. This gingerbread affair was constructed for a San Franciscan lumber baron around 1886.

LEFT AND RIGHT: While some California homes were decidedly gauche, others were true works of art. The Storer House in Los Angeles was one of only four "textile-block" houses built by the architect Frank Lloyd Wright in California, for which he devised an entirely new building technique. Steel rods tied together individually molded concrete blocks, some of which were "pierced" to allow sunlight to enter, and the house was modeled after Mayan designs that suited the California landscape perfectly. Although the style did not catch on, Wright's California homes are lauded as being among the architect's finest.

To say that California was busy in the period beginning with the Gold Rush and the subsequent arrival of the Transcontinental Railroad is a huge understatement. Among the many new towns and cities that date to this period are Chico (founded 1860), Fresno (incorporated 1885), Windsor (first settled 1851), and Garberville (settled 1853). Some—like Stockton—began as mining towns, while others, such as Pacific Grove, began as tourist havens. Still others, Sebastopol for example, were small farming communities that swelled as people drifted away from the mines and tried their hand at agriculture instead. As communities prospered, homes that had often been little more than shacks gave way to the wooden and stone buildings with boarded walks shaded by first floor balconies that will, again, be familiar from Westerns. Meanwhile, the previously sleepy port of Yerba Buena blossomed as a center of trade and banking under its new name of San Francisco. New wealth was spent on ever grander Victorian houses and mansions. Other cities, too, developed their own styles depending on the cultural mix of their inhabitants and the businesses they fostered. For example, Sacramento, which became state capital in 1869, was noticeably more formal in its architecture than other California cities.

Despite the collapse of the first California real estate boom in 1888, over the next century newcomers continued to swell the population, and architecture increasingly reflected different nationalities and personalities. And over the decades those personalities became more flamboyant. Following the example of Mary Pickford and Douglas Fairbanks at the first Hollywood mansion, Pickfair (completed in 1919), movie stars and oil barons built homes that vied to outdo each other in size and glamour and also featured the first swimming pools, which would become a must-have for future generations of well-to-do Californians. Every possible style from Ancient Egyptian to

ABOVE AND BELOW: Among the first of the great mansions built by Hollywood stars and moguls was Pickfair, a twenty-two-room house designed by Wallace Neff for Douglas Fairbanks and Mary Pickford. Reputed to be the first Hollywood home to feature a swimming pool, Pickfair's design was restrained by later standards, but it became the scene of glittering parties attended by visiting European royalty, great writers such as F. Scott Fitzgerald and George Bernard Shaw, and all the movie stars of the silent age.

British Tudor was considered fair game. As the critic Edmund Wilson pointed out in 1931, "Here you will see a Pekinese pagoda made of fresh and crackly peanut brittle—there a snow-white marshmallow igloo—there a toothsome pink nougat in the Florentine manner, rich and delicious with embedded nuts. Yonder rears a clean pocket-size replica of heraldic Warwick Castle—yonder drowses a nausey old nance. . . .And there a hot little hacienda, a regular enchilada conqueso with a roof made of rich red tomato sauce, barely lifts her long-lashed lavender shades on the soul of old Spanish days. . . ."

For those who couldn't afford such opulent—and sometimes tasteless—mansions, there were soon other types of housing available. In 1944 the planned community of San Lorenzo Village in Alameda County became the first of its kind in the nation (and was more famously copied at

ABOVE: The Mission style is a quintessentially California design that has enjoyed many revivals over the years. The smaller windows and shady terraces tend to make for cool interiors well-suited to the climate and landscape.

RIGHT: By the 1920s California was an economic powerhouse, and Signal Hill in Los Angeles County the most productive oil field in the world. The houses built for workers there were typical of those throughout the state. Each was allocated a small plot and was prefabricated in the factory, arriving in easy-to-assemble kit form.

RIGHT: Cheap housing did not necessarily mean loss of comfort. This small house, which cost less than $1,600 to build, was equipped with all the modern features of the day in 1937 and won the Los Angeles architect Harwell Hamilton Harris a national award.

Levittown in New York State). Built for workers in the East Bay district, most of whom were employed in the wartime industries, these houses were cut to size in the factory, quick to construct, comfortable, and cheap. Similar tracts were quickly raised across the state to cope with the continuously booming population.

Despite the welter of styles adopted over the decades, it is possible to point to a few features that became common in California homes, especially in the second half of the twentieth century. Like all good forms of architecture, these have followed the needs and lifestyles of the inhabitants. Due to California's warm climate and spectacular views, by the Fifties and Sixties, houses were borrowing from modernist designs and becoming lighter with bigger windows and sliding doors that allowed inside spaces to become part of the outside. Nevertheless, in a state with weathered beach houses, desert villas, castles, rowhouses, and apartment blocks, it is as difficult to pin down a "typical" architectural style as it is to find a "typical" California family. If the homes of Californians tell us anything about the way they have lived in the past, it is that they are fiercely individualistic people who are as willing to preserve the past as they are to try something new and "crazy." Unlike other places where styles are more rigidly conformed to, California homes perfectly reflect the families that live in them. There's a nonconformist, cheerful, and colorful charm to them that you won't find anywhere else in the world.

ABOVE: A short obelisk marks the site of the Manzanar War Relocation Center. Between 1942 and 1945 Manzanar was the site of one of ten concentration camps where over 110,000 Japanese Americans were interned during World War II. At the foot of the Sierra Nevada, some 230 miles northeast of Los Angeles between Lone Pine and Independence, it was designated a National Historic Site on March 3, 1992, by order of President George H. W. Bush.

RIGHT: Ansel Adams was distressed by the internment and in 1943 produced a photo essay that appeared first as a Museum of Modern Art exhibit. These three images show (right) a Manzanar street scene, (far top right) the view south from Manzanar to Alabama Hills, and (far bottom right) farm workers with Mount Williamson in the background.

HEARST CASTLE

In a state where opulent houses are common, Hearst Castle stands in a league of its own. Built for tycoon William Randolph Hearst between 1919 and 1948 (a difficult man to satisfy, Hearst would often have parts of the house demolished and rebuilt), the fantastic and eccentric mansion is perched in the hills behind San Simeon and surrounded by 127 acres of landscaped gardens. The design of the house itself is based on a Spanish cathedral, but many other architectural styles, from Roman and Egyptian to Medieval British, can be found in parts of the building.

RIGHT: Hearst's beloved home featured fifty-six bedrooms, nineteen sitting rooms, a private theater, indoor and outdoor pools, and the largest private zoo in the world.

LEFT: The imposing grand entrance to Hearst Castle. Throughout, the house was filled with artworks, sculpture, and even an entire ceiling imported from historic and ancient buildings in Europe.

ABOVE: Guests at Hearst Castle included some of the most famous names of the twentieth century, from politicians and royalty to the greatest stars of the day. All would be expected to join Hearst for dinner in the baronial dining hall, but were otherwise free to make use of the house and grounds as they wished.

LEFT: Many Californians will remember birthday parties around the pool, though few were as star-studded as Judy Garland's sixteenth, where guests at Louis B. Mayer's Santa Monica beach home included Mickey Rooney and Ann Rutherford.

BELOW: The homes of the rich and famous in Hollywood became places where they could indulge their fantasies. David Rose, the star of the *Hallmark Playhouse* radio series, installed an entire miniature railroad in his yard. The three model trains, each big enough to haul fifteen children or ten adult passengers, ran on tracks that completely surrounded Rose's Sherman Oaks home and were housed in a depot beside the swimming pool.

BELOW RIGHT: Jayne Mansfield's home featured a heart-shaped pink swimming pool complete with fountains and a mosaic legend on the bottom that read, "I love you Jayne."

OVERLEAF LEFT: In a state where the ostentatious is commonplace, Liberace's home still raised eyebrows. Even the flamboyant singer's marble bathtub cost $55,000.

OVERLEAF RIGHT: By the Fifties many California families, like Johnny Carson's, were enjoying homes that incorporated aspects of modernist design, such as large expanses of glass, which allowed them to make the most of the state's sun and scenery.

ABOVE: The Sixties and Seventies counterculture, along with the clement climate, made California a spiritual home for those who wanted to lead more uncluttered lives. Some families chose to build their own simple houses adding individual ornamentation.

RIGHT: From 1940 onward Frank Lloyd Wright's student John Lautner created a series of classic California homes and buildings across the state that were as innovative as they were beautiful. Among them was the Sheats-Goldstein House of 1963, which took the concept of glass walls to the extreme and has starred in numerous movies since its completion, including *The Big Lebowski* and *Charlie's Angels.*

CALIFORNIA AT PLAY

It's as true now as it was in days gone by that Californians know how to enjoy themselves. California has long been a wealthy state, and many citizens have had the money and the leisure time to indulge their pleasures. California's quickly developing tourist industry has also helped Californians gain a reputation for enjoying themselves. Living in such close proximity to so many tourist facilities and attractions, the natives inevitably took advantage too. The French philosopher and critic Jean Baudrillard saw California as a "resort-style civilization," and looking back it's easy to see why.

In the early years of the Gold Rush, California had an unparalleled reputation as a lawless, licentious state, where amusements were pursued with wild abandon. Although many settlers were upright Victorian folk who would not have dreamed of partaking of such base pleasures, even had they not been too busy carving out a niche for themselves in the wilderness, the state certainly did have

"I love California. Everything out here is fun. There's so many things to do, like go to the mall, go down Melrose. So many places—to the beach. You can basically go anywhere and you'll have fun."

Kristin Herrera

ABOVE: Possibly the most famous cinema in the world, Grauman's Chinese Theatre on Hollywood Boulevard is an amazing fantasy built between 1926 and 1927. Inside are statues specially imported from China and seats for 2,200 customers, while the street outside has the legendary Walk of Fame featuring the handprints and autographs of some of Hollywood's most famous celebrities. The site of countless premieres and parties, Grauman's has also hosted three Academy Award ceremonies.

LEFT: While the first drive-in movie opened in chilly Michigan in 1932, the idea was quickly adopted by California where the weather was more suitable and was soon all the rage. By 1936, drive-ins had opened up and down the state providing cheap, fun entertainment and the perfect venue for a date.

LEFT: For the rich and famous, the Hollywood set provided an endless whirl of parties and balls such as the Mayfair Party at the Beverly Wilshire Hotel in Los Angeles.

bars, brothels, and gambling halls in most towns and cities, often all under the same roof. One early visitor to San Francisco, the Reverend William Taylor, on debarking from his ship in 1849 was moved to write, "It was a scene I shall never forget. On all sides of you were gambling-houses, each with its band of music in full blast. Crowds were going in and out; fortunes were being lost and won, terrible imprecations and blasphemies rose amid the horrid wail, and it seemed to me that Pandemonium was let loose." This was a common enough scene in San Francisco in those heady days, and as the decades passed California would retain its reputa-

OPPOSITE: The stars of the forties and fifties often retreated for breaks at the select resorts of Palm Springs, such as Normandy Village, where relaxed parties could be held in the desert surroundings well out of sight of gawking tourists and gossip columnists.

ABOVE: For the ordinary folk of Los Angeles who wanted a little privacy, a favorite date was parking at one of the frequent "make out" points on scenic Mulholland Drive.

tion for high living. Some parts of the state would become infamous for their decadence, particularly Los Angeles, where gossip columnists would later fill their pages with tales of Hollywood excess much as they do today.

While such hedonism is a part of California lore, it represents just the extreme. Away from the bawdy houses, California offered numerous more modest and healthy ways for natives and tourists alike to enjoy themselves, even in the early years. Pacific Grove was founded as a summer camp for devout Methodists in 1875, but by 1890 had become a haven for artists, while less creative tourists delighted in the sun, sea, and scenery. In 1864 Yosemite became the first area in the United States to become protected parkland on the passage of the Yosemite Grant, signed by Abraham Lincoln. Giant redwoods of the sequoia forests were also

OPPOSITE AND ABOVE: The jitterbug craze swept the nation in the 1930s and nowhere did people dance to the great swing bands of the time more enthusiastically than California. At the time hepcats and their girls would dance anywhere, any time, from a morning charity event to an afternoon dance-off on the beach.

a popular item on the itineraries of California's first tourists as were the fledgling vineyards of Napa Valley. One of the first visitors to take a wine sampling tour was the British author of *Treasure Island*, Robert Louis Stevenson, who spent his honeymoon among the vines in 1880. Another tourist attraction were the natural springs of Death Valley. These were thought to have curative powers and by the 1930s there were thriving resorts in the desert. There was also the famous vacation home of Chicago millionaire couple Albert and Bessie Johnson, Scotty's Castle, so named for the local and colorful character who conned them out of a small fortune but also became their friend. It was a favorite getaway for celebrities and movie stars in the 1930s. By the following decade Palm Springs had become a sunny vacation spot for wealthy Californians and tourists alike, while on the coast surfing was introduced in the early twentieth century and gained in popularity over the following decades at resorts and beachfront towns along the Pacific shore.

As you might expect, many Californians over the years took great pleasure in the outdoor pursuits the state offers. The sun

ABOVE: In an effort to attract customers, diners up and down the state adopted some very strange designs from the 1920s onward. The Zep Diner in Los Angeles was positively restrained compared to the Bulldog Diner in Beverly Hills (shaped, of course, like an enormous bulldog).

and natural features make it a great place for outdoor sports and pastimes of all sorts, from simple daily pleasures such as barbecueing, baseball in the yard, or beach volleyball to more adventurous fun such as rock climbing, camping in the thick pine forests, whitewater rafting, or hiking in the deserts and mountains. Every Californian will have fond memories of balmy evenings outdoors serenaded by cicadas, nights at the local drive-in (the first drive-in to open in California was Los Angeles's Pico in 1934), or parking with a date.

Yet there are also more refined enjoyments to be had. The state's first permanent theater was the tiny Eagle Theatre in Sacramento, which dates to as early as 1855. Here, prospectors would expect rougher entertainments than their cousins back east, but over the years California has grown to offer world class theaters, opera houses, and concert halls. The San Francisco War Memorial Opera House, for example, staged its first performance (*La Bohème*) in 1923. And of course, there was always the movies. The movie capital of the world became a showcase for palatial and exotic theaters. The most famous is Grauman's Chinese Theatre in Los

ABOVE: Outdoor games and sports have always been popular with young Californians, and few more so than baseball. The state has produced some of the nation's greatest ballplayers over the years, little wonder when children could practice in the yard with dad all year-round.

Angeles, which has been welcoming audiences and staging premieres since 1927, but there are numerous examples of equally fantastic cinemas around the state, such as the fabulous art deco Paramount Theatre in Oakland.

Any visitor today could be forgiven for thinking that the state is one huge playground, boasting theme parks and theaters, casinos, exclusive resorts, and

ABOVE: California counts some of the United States' most beautiful national parks among its attractions, with trees such as the large western juniper that would have been saplings at the height of the Roman Empire 2,000 years ago, as well as abundant wildlife and spectacular views. With all this available, hiking has been popular since the earliest tourists arrived in the mid-nineteenth century and by 1965 was a favorite weekend jaunt for scouts.

restaurants of every imaginable cuisine, not to mention aquariums, museums, and events ranging from the great San Francisco Jazz Festival to the (much recommended) Oakhurst Fall Chocolate and Wine Festival. With all this to offer, as well as sandy beaches, who can blame us for wanting to enjoy the delights on our doorsteps? Whether our preferred entertainment is a fire-lit beach party after a day's surfing or a grand opera, we Californians seem to have joie de vivre written into our genetic code.

TOP LEFT AND LEFT: The Sierra Nevada provides some of the nation's best skiing and is easily accessible to most Californians. (The lowest and highest points of the United States are both in California and within 100 miles of each other, with Bad Water in Death Valley being 282 feet below sea level and Mount Whitney 14,495 feet above it.) Although the first recorded account of skiing in the state dates back to 1873, the Big Pines Park was the first official winter playground and opened in 1924. By the Thirties there were numerous ski resorts, many of which held an annual Snow Carnival.

ABOVE: The psychedelic years of the Sixties provided California's hippies, as well as anyone else who happened to be passing, with some great entertainment. Street performances of mime, theater, and music were common and admission was free.

OPPOSITE: The legendary rock club, Whisky a Go Go on Sunset Boulevard, was America's first discotheque when it opened in 1958. Featuring a short-skirted D.J. suspended in a cage and live music from acts such as Johnny Rivers and, later, the Doors, the Whisky is widely believed to be the birthplace of rock 'n' roll in California. Still going strong after more than half a century, the club has been celebrated in song as well as showcasing some of the greatest bands of the twentieth century, from punk stars like Iggy Pop to the heavy rock of Guns n' Roses.

United Artists Records
Hollywood, Calif.
TO: Paul Anka
Greek Theatre
Los Angeles, Calif. AUG. 4-9
SPECIAL DELIVERY
FOSTER and KLEISER
el Grande de Coca-Cola
El Grande de Coca-Cola
SHELL
Whisky a Go Go
THE FUNNIEST SHOW IN TOWN
EL GRANDE DE
COCA COLA
TICKETS AVAILABLE NOW
Beautiful Loser
A New Album By
59.9 SHELL REGULAR
61.9 SUPER REGULAR
63.9 SUPER SHELL
GASOLINE
MAPS to STARS HOMES
National

BEACH LIFE

With nearly 1,000 miles of beaches, year-round sunshine, and over 50 percent of Californians living within 50 miles of the shore, it's easy to understand why the state has had such an enduring love affair with the beach. There are no accurate figures for how many people visit the beach each year, though it is estimated to be several hundred million. But there is no doubt at all that over the years California's beaches have provided locals and visitors with enduring memories and a lot of good times.

BELOW AND RIGHT: The forerunner of waterskiing was aquaplaning, and by the 1920s Californians had taken to the sport as only Californians could, inventing new games and stunts that showed off their prowess on every stretch of water from Lake Tahoe to the Pacific. The game of Aquaplane Ball, being demonstrated (below) at Catalina Island, involved keeping the ball in the air as long as possible. Any player who allowed it to drop was "out" and their penalty was to swim back for the ball.

ABOVE: With typical California inventiveness, the girls of Venice Beach find a new use for beach umbrellas and brooms.

ABOVE: The sun-kissed teenagers of Santa Monica enjoy California's favorite pastime during the last days of summer on Labor Day 1961.

ABOVE: While we may not all have had Corvette Stingrays, this scene will be familiar to many Californians who grew up driving to the beach with their date to surf and hang out with friends on the sands.

SPORTING CALIFORNIA

"They throw the ball, I hit it; they hit the ball, I catch it."

Willie Mays of the San Francisco Giants

RIGHT: Built for the much-loved minor league team the San Francisco Seals at a cost of $100,000, Ewing Field opened on May 16, 1914, and was possibly California's least successful ballpark. Famous for becoming fog-bound during games, most Seals fans lived in the Mission, which was too far to travel. When the team was sold to the Los Angeles Angels in 1915, the new owners announced that the Seals would never again play in the park.

With nineteen major league sports franchises—more than any other state—California is home to some of the nation's greatest teams in every sport from football and baseball to ice hockey and soccer. More major league baseball players have been raised here than any other state, including greats such as Jackie Robinson, Joe DiMaggio, Ted Williams, and Tom Seaver. California has also fielded legendary football teams including the Oakland Raiders teams of the mid-1960s and the San Francisco 49ers of the 1980s. The state's universities have long fostered sports programs and its athletes are often ranked nationally, while the state is also the first to have hosted a college bowl game—the Rose Bowl, which dates back to 1902. Even its youngest players have seen fierce competition on the ball field for decades. Over the years California has hosted the Summer Olympics twice in Los Angeles (in 1932 and 1984) as well as a Winter Olympics at Squaw Valley Ski Resort in 1960, and the Olympic-style California State Games have been a much loved fixture on the calendar for the last twenty years. Outside of the stadiums, ballparks, and arenas, Californians have adopted and developed just about every sport imaginable, from sailing and surfing to kayaking and volleyball. California loves sport.

Like many other states, California has

ABOVE: Sadly demolished in the 1950s, Washington Park in Los Angeles was the home of the Los Angeles Angels from 1912 to 1925. While it didn't have the seating capacity of later ballparks, it was held in great esteem by spectators.

BELOW: Los Angeles Olympic Stadium on opening day of the Games of the Xth Olympiad, in 1932. Due to the Great Depression only thirty-seven countries attended, but California delivered an exciting Games during which the athletes of the United States were triumphant. The final tally of U.S. gold medals amounted to forty-one, while Italy came in second with just twelve.

LEFT: Like colleges across the nation, Whittier College has been fielding teams for various sports for over a century. Among them was the 1933 women's hockey team, who defeated all opposition on their home field.

a proud baseball heritage. As in so many other areas of its history, the state can trace its ball playing roots back to the Gold Rush. Along with many other items of cultural baggage brought to the west by the Forty-Niners was the new game of Base Ball (the first ball field had been devised in New York only a few years previously in 1845 by Alexander Joy Cartwright). The game was popular, though for the first few years local teams were prevented from competing outside the state by the long and arduous journey. But the Transcontinental Railroad also brought with it teams from farther away, like the Cincinnati Red Stockings, who were the first to visit in 1869 and inspired the local teams with displays of flair and professionalism. By 1903, California was part of the Pacific Coast League along with the northwestern states, but it wasn't until a half century later that the state acquired its first major league teams. Appropriately, New York supplied them. Both the Brooklyn Dodgers and New York Giants transferred to California in 1958, becoming the Los Angeles Dodgers and the San Francisco Giants. As any San Franciscan will tell you, the Giants hold the distinction of having won more games than any other team in sporting history.

OPPOSITE, TOP AND BOTTOM: Southern California's oldest horse racing track, Santa Anita, opened in 1934 and has witnessed some great racing over the years, including Seabiscuit's amazing win of the 1940 Santa Anita Handicap (bottom), the last race of the famous horse's legendary career. The track has also starred in a number of movies, including the Marx Brothers classic, *A Day at the Races*.

Football came slightly later with the first games being played in eastern American colleges during the 1870s. The game was quickly adopted by California and over the years the state has seen more than its fair share of victory. The Golden Bears college teams of the 1920s gave the state its first golden years of football by going five years and fifty games between 1920 and 1925 without suffering a single defeat. By the middle of the century, the state had teams including the San Francisco 49ers (formed in 1946) and the Los Angeles Chargers (now the San Diego Chargers) who began playing in 1960. A surprise team was founded in 1960 when an AFL franchise was unexpectedly given to Oakland, and the Oakland Raiders were formed.

WIN 137360 POOL
PLACE 108693 POOL
SHOW 136647 POOL
TOTE TICKETS PAY
TIME
JOCKEY CHANGES AND OVERWEIGHTS

LEFT: Baseball has provided a distraction through bad times as well as good in California. Taken by the great photographer Ansel Adams, this picture shows the Manzanar Relocation Center, where some of the 110,000 California citizens of Japanese descent were imprisoned during World War II.

With its new teams to house and fans to satisfy, California began building ballparks and stadiums. And like the rest of the state, California's are a little different from anything you would find elsewhere. Fans from out of state are often incredulous that alongside the traditional hot dogs you can also get cappuccino, fish tacos, and sushi! Dodger Stadium opened at Chavez Ravine in Los Angeles in 1962, and until 1995 was the only National League park apart from Wrigley Field in Chicago to be used solely for baseball. Over the years it has seen some great action, including eight World Series, was voted the best ballpark by major league players in 2003, and has become a treasured landmark for millions of baseball fans. The Giants found their own new home at Candlestick Park in San Francisco, which opened in 1960 and also

RIGHT: While Candlestick Park is one of California's favorite ballparks, fans will remember the winds that created odd playing conditions there, on one occasion blowing pitcher Stu Miller off balance during the first All Star Game in 1961, and the fact that the heating never did work.

RIGHT: In the days before the Gold Rush, the great California sport was the rodeo, a tradition that continues to this day on the ProRodeo Circuit. In the days of the ranchos, early Spanish Californians were probably the finest horsemen in the world and never missed a chance to pit their incredible riding and roping skills against each other. As the years passed the vaqueros' horsemanship was passed on to a generation of cowboys, and impromptu competitions sprang up around the United States, particularly after it was realized that people would pay to watch. Californians have become firm fans since the early twentieth century and the town of Salinas has been a major stop on the pro rodeo circuit since a Wild West Show was held there in 1911. The Livermore Rodeo of 1946 saw Pete Dixon bareback-riding Peppery Red Pepper to a big money win.

ABOVE: Pictured here iin 1955, the twentieth annual Flight of the Snowbirds, a race for small sailing craft at Newport Harbor. In that year 135 "salts" took to the water, though only 115 finished.

became the home ground of the Oakland Raiders in 1961 and the San Francisco 49ers in 1971. Like most stadiums and ballparks, Candlestick also hosted numerous other events and has a place in history as the venue of the last-ever Beatles concert in 1966. While these two grand dames were the first major league grounds, they weren't the last and California soon had more great new teams with stadiums of their own, including Oakland Coliseum (home to the Oakland Raiders and Oakland Athletics), Anaheim Stadium (the home field of the Los Angeles/California Angels and Los Angeles Rams), and Jack Murphy Stadium in San Diego (home of the San Diego Padres and San Diego Chargers).

The other great California sport is—of course—surfing, which in California has something of a royal heritage. The first three people to take to the waves in the state were Hawaiian princes who fashioned their boards from local redwood in

1885. The sport gradually caught on over the ensuing decades, and by the 1930s there were numerous surf clubs up and down the coast. The first West Coast Surfing Championship dates back to 1959 at Huntington Beach. These days it's a rare Californian who has never at least tried to catch a wave.

With typical inclusiveness the state has also pioneered women's sports, regularly fields competitors in the Special Olympics, and was also home to the first gay rodeo in 1975. Its snowboarders and skiers regularly compete on an international level, and it is also the heartland for football of another kind: Soccer has been popular here since the Los Angeles Kickers club was formed in 1955. As noted in the previous chapter, Californians love to enjoy themselves, and for many the greatest thrills around are sporting ones. To explore all the events and competitions that California has excelled at over the years would need far more space than is available here, but some of the images that follow might stir some memories.

LEFT: California has fielded some of the greatest names in sport, but few in the league of Magic Johnson, who played for the Los Angeles Lakers from 1979 until he retired in 1991 (though he came out of retirement to play numerous more games with the Lakers). Gold medalist at the 1992 Olympics and named one of the fifty greatest players in NBA history, Johnson became a national hero.

ABOVE: Behind every great team is an even better cheerleading squad, and California has laid claim to the best, from the world-famous Laker Girls to the Los Angeles Rams Cheerleaders, formerly known as the "Embraceable Ewes."

ABOVE: World Figure Skating Champion Carol Heiss of New York City at the Squaw Valley practice rink of the 1960 Winter Olympics where she later took the gold medal.

TOP RIGHT: Over the years, California has witnessed world championships in sports of all descriptions, including the 1978 Frisbee World Championships at Santa Monica.

RIGHT: Willie Mays, San Francisco Giants legend, slides into home plate safely during a game against the New York Mets in 1964.

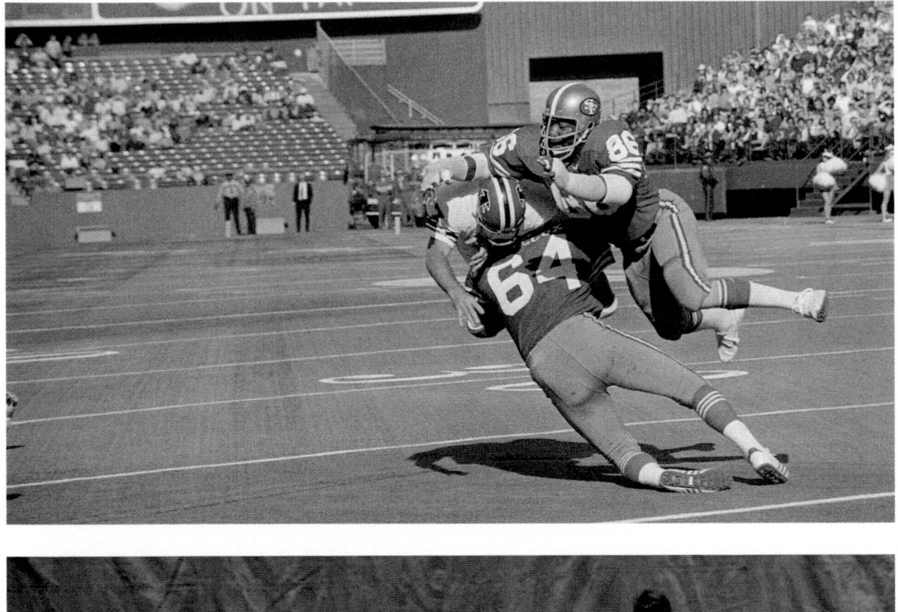

LEFT: The San Francisco 49ers play at their home ground against the Atlanta Falcons November 24, 1974, with Cedrick Hardman (86) and Dave Wilcox taking down Falcon Pat Sullivan during a game the 49ers would eventually win 27–0.

LEFT: Winner of twelve Grand Slam singles titles, sixteen Grand Slam doubles titles, and eleven Grand Slam mixed doubles titles, as well as winning the famous "Battle of the Sexes" match against Wimbledon champion Bobby Riggs, Long Beach native Billie Jean King is undoubtedly California's greatest tennis player.

THE ROSE BOWL

With a history dating back over a century, the annual postseason college football game at the Rose Bowl in Pasadena has become a beloved New Year tradition. Known as the "Tournament East-West Football Game" when it was first played as part of the Tournament of Roses festival in 1902, the Stanford University team was given such a beating by Michigan (49–0 with Stanford ceding victory in the third quarter) that the game wasn't played again until 1916. Since then, however, it has attracted more spectators than any other college football game and has acquired the nickname "The Grandaddy of Them All."

RIGHT: A record Rose Bowl crowd of 102,946 saw the University of Southern California win over Indiana University 14–3 in the 54th Rose Bowl football game on January 1, 1968.

BELOW LEFT: Now a National Historic Landmark, the Rose Bowl first hosted the game on January 1, 1923, the same day it was officially dedicated. The game has been held here every year since, with the exception of 1942 when it was considered too dangerous following the bombing of Pearl Harbor.

ABOVE: Sam "the Man" Cunningham shows the form that led him to a new Rose Bowl record of four touchdowns in a single game. Cunningham scored four touchdowns against the Ohio State Buckeyes, all by diving over the goal line and a strongly assembled defense set to stop him. The USC Trojans ran all over the Ohio State Buckeyes and won the 1973 Rose Bowl by a score of 42–17.

LEFT: A packed crowd attends the Big Game between Stanford and the University of California at Berkeley at the California Memorial Stadium on the Berkeley campus, November 20, 1926. With a history dating back to 1892 (at which time the Stanford manager was Herbert Hoover), the annual game has become the state's biggest event in college football with winners being awarded the Stanford Axe.

ABOVE: Douglas Fairbanks, Jr., (left), Douglas Fairbanks, and Mary Pickford attend the Pittsburgh–Southern California football classic on January 1, 1933.

A SPECIAL PLACE

Mardi Gras in San Diego's historic Gaslamp Quarter; dinner on the stunning art deco *Queen Mary* moored at Long Beach; the Fourth of July Parade at Huntington Beach; Van Gogh at the Richard Meier–designed Getty Center in Los Angeles; hiking at Big Sur and the surf breaks at Santa Cruz; the annual Bay to Breakers foot race held in San Francisco since 1912; a glass of locally produced wine in Santa Rosa; Blues on the Bay in Eureka, country music in Bakersfield, or the Fresno Grand Opera; the amazing sequoias of Redwood National Park…

The list of what makes California special could go on and on. Every time you think you may have gotten the measure of this state you will find something else to startle you. As people have been finding for many years, this is no New York or Texas or New England, where—wonderful as those states might be—things are more or less as you'd expect from town to town. California specializes in doing

"In California in the early Spring, There are pale yellow mornings, when the mist burns slowly into day, The air stings like Autumn, clarifies like pain — Well, I have dreamed this coast myself."

Robert Hass

ABOVE: Located 22 miles off the southwest coast of Los Angeles, Santa Catalina Island has been a popular resort since the late 1800s. Visitors to Catalina can always enjoy good music. Whether it is a spirited dance at the Pavilion (pictured) or relaxing to the smooth sounds of the annual Catalina Island Jazztrax Festival, this small paradise has it all.

ABOVE: Admiring the view from Overhanging Rock in Yosemite National Park in 1901. The massive granite crest of Half Dome is visible on the left. In the 1870s the great summit was declared "perfectly inaccessible" until George Anderson scaled its peak in 1875.

ABOVE: For many, California has always been synonymous with the rich and, more important, the famous. More than any other place on the planet, it offers the dream of, if not actual celebrity, then the chance to get closer to it. Taken in 1936, this photograph illustrates that dream was just as powerful then as it is today.

ABOVE: Saint Patrick's Day celebrations in Sacramento begin with an early morning shave. This mass grooming session is the kick-off for a whisker growing competition where each contestant forgoes shaving until the last week in May. The goal is to look as much like a pioneer as possible in readiness for the Spring Festival.

ABOVE: Former mayor of Fresno and owner of the famous Pony Express Museum in San Marino, W. Parker Lyon stands behind a bar from the old mining camp of Mariposa, California. The museum holds the largest collection of relics dating back to the Gold Rush and the original Pony Express.

things differently. Los Angeles may be a crazy glamour city where looks alone can get you far, but Berkeley more than makes up for it with its leafy air of academia. Far to the north the old fishing town of Crescent City might get 70 inches of rainfall a year, but balmy San Diego rarely sees more than 10. From town to town and scene to scene, California is full of dramatic changes and delicious surprises.

The people, too, are different here. Over the years many have remarked on it. The writer Edward Abbey once famously said, "There is science, logic, reason; there is thought verified by experience. And then there is California." He was right. California has a state of mind that is unlike any other part of the United States. Fundamentally American, California was nevertheless long cut off from the rest of the continent and, with the Sierra Nevada at its back, looks out over the Pacific. The cultural mix is richer here than anywhere in the United States and in the early years the state was far from the laws and social strictures of the East, giving a sense of freedom that has been passed down through generations. Californians have always delighted in their individuality and the sense that this is a place where any-

LEFT: Displaying a dizzying lack of fear, these workers on the Golden Gate Bridge in San Francisco are constructing a catwalk that connects to each of the towers, enabling them to attach the necessary cables. On its completion in 1937, it was the longest suspension bridge in the world and its unique design quickly made it an immediately recognizable symbol of California.

RIGHT: The alluring actresses Marilyn Monroe and Jane Russell immortalize their handprints on Hollywood's Walk of Fame outside Grauman's Chinese Theatre in 1953. There are now nearly 200 handprints, footprints, and autographs embedded in the concrete outside the theater.

thing can happen. Perhaps too, the ever-present threat of earthquakes means that the people here tend to live for the moment. Sometimes this manifests itself in a certain craziness. You only have to look at the buildings to know that Californians can be given to flights of fancy. Often though, it results in great bursts of creative brilliance and innovation: great works of engineering such as the Golden Gate Bridge or the music of the Beach Boys or the Doors. Californians have achieved more in just over a century and a half than those of other states have in double the time.

As with any place, California has been shaped by its environment and history. Looking back, it's not difficult to see how it has become slightly unlike the rest of the nation. Other states—Florida or Louisiana, for example—have a strong Spanish heritage, but nowhere did this develop in such isolation from the rest of the country. And while gold has been unearthed elsewhere, the Gold Rush of 1849 has become lodged in popular culture. Few places have enjoyed such a bounty of natural blessings, giving California an enviable industrial and agricultural wealth as well as making it a favorite destination for tourists. Hollywood too has played its part. The sights and sounds

BELOW: The real life "Rocket Man," Peter Kedzierski makes a spectacular entrance to the opening of the California State Fair of 1962. Typifying the true California spirit of adventure combined with no small amount of showmanship, the Rocket Man was one of the most popular attractions of the twelve-day event.

of California played out on celluloid around the world as it grew up, making the state the world's crucible of popular culture.

California is all of this and more. It is sleepy groves of orange trees and small towns with white picket fences. It is works of great architecture and whimsical buildings such as Bakersfield's Big Shoe. It is atmospheric old diners and art deco movie theaters, deserts, forests, valleys, and beaches. It is Fifties signage on old Route 66 and rock 'n' roll. What makes California special is not its history, or the roads, rails, and industry. It's not Disneyland or wineries, the architecture or the sports grounds, or even the sunshine. It is the sum of all of these things and the amazing memories that have been created here.

OPPOSITE: Schwab's Drug Store on Sunset Boulevard enjoyed the patronage of many movie actors and executives between the 1930s and the 1950s, earning itself the nickname of "Headquarters" to those in the know. It was also home to one of the most popular "discovery" myths in Hollywood. Legend had it that Lana Turner was spotted here by William R. Wilkerson, who referred her to Zeppo Marx thus catapulting her into a successful movie career. She was actually discovered in the Top Hat Café, over a mile away.

ABOVE: Perhaps the most famous broken sign in the world, the original "Hollywoodland" advertisement was initially erected to promote a new housing development in the Hollywood Hills. Each letter was 30 feet wide and 50 feet high and covered with 4,000 light bulbs. What was supposed to be a temporary fixture was quickly embraced by the populace and is now a protected landmark.

LEFT: The hauntingly barren landscape of Death Valley has become a de facto star in its own right. The striking scenery has appeared in countless movies, novels, and television shows. Immense, inhospitable yet dazzling, Death Valley is a place like no other.

ABOVE: There are few sights that bring to mind so forcibly an image of San Francisco than the cable car. Although now mainly used as a tourist attraction, the cars still operate limited routes and work has begun on improving the system.

LEFT: California in the Sixties has always been viewed by the outside world as a place of vibrant colors and exuberant characters. This conglomeration of artists and clothing designers are celebrating the reopening of the newly painted Aquarius Theater in 1969. This venue would later host such legends as The Doors and become the venue for the iconic musical *Hair*.

BELOW: One of the most successful and influential artists of the "folk rock" movement in the early Seventies, Joni Mitchell plays the autoharp for a young girl at her house in Laurel Canyon, California.

ABOVE: The usually balmy weather of San Francisco is interrupted by a spectacular lightning storm. The sweeping view from Diamond Heights shows the electrical bombardment of the downtown district.

OPPOSITE: The Antelope Valley California Poppy Reserve blossoms into life. During the blooming season the bright orange flowers carpet the entire 1,745 acres of parkland. The official flower of California, the poppy can be seen on the welcome signs posted at California's borders, and April 6th has been declared California Poppy Day.

RIGHT: Opened in 1928 and named after the highway it stood beside, Café 101 is the oldest restaurant in Oceanside, California. When the highway was relocated, the owner of Café 101 had the foresight and acumen to change the restaurant into a drive-in and later a coffee shop. It has only recently reverted to its original name and remains a firm favorite with tourists and locals.

References in **bold** refer to illustrations.